7/07

Famous Places of the World

Europe

Helen Bateman and Jayne Denshire

Smart Apple Media

This edition first published in 2006 in the United States of America by Smart Apple Media.

Smart Apple Media
2140 Howard Drive West
North Mankato
Minnesota 56003

First published in 2006 by
MACMILLAN EDUCATION AUSTRALIA PTY LTD
627 Chapel Street, South Yarra, Australia 3141

Visit our Web site at www.macmillan.com.au

Associated companies and representatives throughout the world.

Library of Congress Cataloging-in-Publication Data

Bateman, Helen.
  Europe / by Helen Bateman and Jayne Denshire.
    p. cm. — (Famous places of the world)
  Includes index.
  ISBN-13: 978-1-58340-803-2 (alk. paper)
  1. Europe—Description and travel—Juvenile literature. 2. Historic sites—Europe—Juvenile
  literature. I. Denshire, Jayne. II. Title.

  D910.5.B38 2006
  940—dc22   2006002522

Project management by Limelight Press Pty Ltd
Design by Stan Lamond, Lamond Art & Design
Illustrations by Marjorie Crosby-Fairall
Maps by Lamond Art & Design and Andrew Davies
Map icons by Andrew Davies
Research by Kate McAllan
Consultant: Colin Sale BA (Sydney) MSc (London)

Printed in USA

Acknowledgments
The authors and the publisher are grateful to the following for permission to reproduce copyright material:

Cover photograph: The Colosseum, Rome, courtesy of iStockphoto/Steve Geer.
APL p. 23; APL/Jason Hawkes p. 14; APL/Sandro Vannini p. 13; GettyImages/Grant Faint p. 27; GettyImages/Robert Frerck p. 10; iStockphoto/Eric Armstrong p. 25(top left); iStockphoto/Michael Blackburn p. 4 (right); iStockphoto/Bryan Busovicki p. 15; iStockphoto/Marc-André Decoste p. 6; iStockphoto/Jean-Claude Gallard p. 11 (top left); iStockphoto/Debi Gardiner p. 4 (center left); iStockphoto/Steve Geer p. 22; iStockphoto/Melissa Jewart p. 18; iStockphoto/Marco Radtke p. 17 (top left); iStockphoto/Tomasz Resiak p. 4 (left); iStockphoto/Margaret Smeaton p. 4 (center right); iStockphoto/Craig Stanton p. 12; iStockphoto/Evgeny Zimin p. 28; Lonely Planet/Graham Bell p. 29 (top left); Lonely Planet/Jon Davison p. 19; Lonely Planet/Donald C. & Priscilla Alexander Eastman p. 11 (center right); Lonely Planet/John Elk III p. 8; Lonely Planet/Mark Honan p. 7; Lonely Planet/ David Peevers p. 21; Lonely Planet/Damien Simonis p. 25 (center right); Lonely Planet/Jonathan Smith pp. 16, 17 (center right), 29 (center right); PhotoDisc pp. 24, 26; Photolibrary.com/Jon Arnold p. 9; Photolibrary.com/Walter Bibikow p. 20.

Contents

When a word in the text is printed in **bold**. You can look up its meaning in the Glossary on page 31.

Wonders of Europe

Europe is a small **continent** that consists of 43 countries. Each country has its own culture and, in most cases, its own language. There are many famous places in Europe. Some are ancient and some are modern. Most of Europe's famous places have been built by humans, but it is also home to many natural wonders.

What makes a place famous?

The most common reasons why places become famous are because of their:

- **formation** how they were formed by nature
- **construction** how they were built by humans
- **antiquity** their age, dating back to ancient times
- **size** their height, width, length, volume, or area
- **function** how they work, or what they are used for
- **cultural importance** their value to the customs and society of the country
- **religious importance** their value to the religious beliefs of the country

ZOOM IN
Europe is the second smallest continent in the world.

4

Famous places in Europe

Europe has many famous places. Some are built structures and some are features created by nature.

Key

Eiffel Tower	Mont Blanc	Roman Baths	The City of Venice
Little Mermaid	Stonehenge	Danube River	Parthenon
Alhambra	Brandenburg Gate	Colosseum	Kremlin

Eiffel Tower

The Eiffel Tower is a built structure that is famous for its construction and cultural importance. It was one of the first steel and **wrought-iron** towers ever built. It soon became the symbol of Paris throughout the world.

The tower is named after Gustave Eiffel whose engineers designed it. The design won a competition held to commemorate the **centenary** of the French Revolution that took place in 1789.

Tower construction

The Eiffel Tower consists of four massive **pylons** constructed from **girders**. The pylons are joined together at the top of the tower. The tower was made in sections in Eiffel's factory, and then brought to the site and put together there.

ZOOM IN

The Eiffel Tower is painted in a slightly different grey each time to help painters know which bits they have already painted.

◄ The Eiffel Tower is made of metal, so it shrinks in the cold weather, and swells in the hot weather. The tower can vary by about 6 inches (15 cm).

► The Eiffel Tower needs constant repair and care. It is first painted with a special paint to stop the metal from rusting.

Open design

The tower's open design allows the wind to pass through it. This means that it is able to withstand strong winds. Each of the tower's legs stands on a concrete base. Because the foundations go underground, the men who built them worked in underground, watertight **chambers**. The building of the Eiffel Tower is famous for being one of the greatest engineering achievements of the 1800s.

▼ The Eiffel Tower took only just over two years to complete. The foundations were laid in January, 1888 and the final platform was completed in May, 1889.

| April, 1888 | August, 1888 | March, 1889 | May, 1889 |

Little Mermaid

The Little Mermaid is a built monument that is famous for its construction and its cultural importance. It was sculpted in bronze by Danish sculptor Edvard Eriksen, who modeled the statue on his wife. It is recognized as the symbol of Denmark throughout the world.

▼ The sculpture shows the very moment of the story of the Little Mermaid when her tail is transforming into legs.

INSIDE STORY

The Little Mermaid was written by Hans Christian Andersen in 1836. It tells the story of a mermaid who falls in love with a prince who lives on land. The Sea Witch sells the Little Mermaid a magic drink. This grants her human legs and a life on land in exchange for her beautiful voice and her life in the sea. But the magic drink makes every step she takes on land painful. Eventually the Little Mermaid accepts that she cannot live on the land and cannot return to the sea. She is turned into a spirit and joins the spirit world.

ZOOM IN

The statue was commissioned by a rich businessman after he saw a ballet of Hans Christian Andersen's story, *The Little Mermaid*.

► The Little Mermaid sits on the shoreline, on the edge of the land and the sea. In the famous story, too, she does not really belong to either the land or the sea.

Famous writer

The statue is a monument to Hans Christian Andersen, one of Denmark's most famous writers. It represents his fairy tale, *The Little Mermaid*, one of his most famous stories.

By the sea

The statue of the Little Mermaid was set on a rock on the seashore so that she could always be wet, like a real mermaid. It sits staring out at the sea. The sculpture illustrates the part of the fairy tale just before the Little Mermaid changes into a human.

The Little Mermaid has been deliberately damaged a number of times and has been successfully repaired each time. The Danish Government has taken precautions so that its most famous monument will not be damaged again.

ZOOM IN
The sculptor made a mold of the Little Mermaid, so if a part is damaged, it can be easily remade and reattached.

Alhambra

FACT FINDER

Location **Granada, Spain**

Date built **1238–1527**

**WORLD HERITAGE SITE
since 1984**

The Alhambra is a built structure that is famous for its construction and its cultural and religious importance. This palace was first built as a fortress with massive red brick walls and high towers. Inside the walls, the chambers, gardens and courtyards are some of the greatest examples of Islamic architecture in the world.

Three sections

The Alhambra palace is made up of three sections. Each is a series of rooms arranged around a courtyard. This design fits in with the Muslim tradition of building homes around courtyards to gain privacy and to block out the outside world. Some of the courtyards were open to the public. Others were for the private use of the **sultans**, or rulers, who lived in Spain from the 1200s to the 1500s.

▼ The palace was built and decorated according to Muslim traditions and culture.

▲ Writings from the Koran, the holy book of Islam, are carved as decorations on the walls and ceilings.

The buildings

The buildings are made mainly of brick, cement and concrete. The palace floors are covered in marble, and the walls are decorated with ceramic tiles and wood. Many of the wall decorations feature religious sayings and passages from the Koran, the holy book of Islam.

The Alhambra palace is famous for achieving a relationship and balance between the buildings, decorations, water and gardens. This balance supports the Muslim idea of a perfect world, or paradise.

▲ The Court of the Lions was an area for the sultan and his family to have private gatherings.

ZOOM IN

The name of the complex comes from the very first building, the Arabic *Qal' at al-Hamra*, which means "The Red Fortress."

Mont Blanc

FACT FINDER

Location France, Italy and Switzerland

Height 15,771 feet (4,807 m)

Width 10 miles (16 km)

Mont Blanc is a natural landform that is famous for its size. It is the tallest mountain in the Alps and in western Europe. Its height varies from year to year, depending on the snowfall. It has been recorded at 15,781 feet (4,810 m) after heavy snowfalls.

ZOOM IN
A 6-mile (11-km) tunnel has been built under the mountain. It links France and Italy.

▼ In summer, there is not much snow on the lower slopes of Mont Blanc. In winter, they are covered in thick snow. Near the peak there is always snow.

► The Mer de Glace glacier is the largest glacier on the mountain. It flows slowly down the mountain.

White mountain

Mont Blanc, which is French for "white mountain," is a massive block of granite that extends into three countries. The borders of France, Italy, and Switzerland all meet on the mountain, although France claims to own the **summit**.

Forests and streams

The lower slopes of Mont Blanc have thick forests and fast-flowing streams. Higher areas have little **vegetation**, and the highest are covered in snow all year round. Rivers of snow and ice, which are called **glaciers**, flow slowly down the mountain from the summit. The ice that melts at the bottom is replaced by more snowfalls at the top. The most famous glacier is the Mer de Glace, which is French for "sea of ice." The glaciers scrape Mont Blanc's rocky sides and carry soil and broken rock away. This world-famous mountain is being slowly worn down by the action of the flowing ice.

ZOOM IN
Recently, the Mer de Glace glacier was estimated to have moved 148 feet (45 m) in one year.

Stonehenge

FACT FINDER

Location **Salisbury, England, United Kingdom**

Date built **3100–2000 B.C.**

WORLD HERITAGE SITE since 1986

Stonehenge is a built structure that is famous for its construction and its antiquity. Today, Stonehenge is a collection of stone slabs arranged in a circular pattern. Inside the circle, more stones are arranged in the shape of a horseshoe. Today's Stonehenge was built about 4,000 years ago.

ZOOM IN
Some historians say that the bluestone rocks were brought to Stonehenge by sea on rafts and by land on a system of rollers.

▼ The stones that stand today form an outer circle with a horseshoe shape inside.

Three stages of construction

Stonehenge was built in three stages. The first stage began around 5,000 years ago with a circular ditch containing earth, stone, and wooden structures. The second stage began about 4,200 years ago when huge bluestone slabs were moved to the site from Wales, more than 185 miles (300 km) away. The third stage consisted of sandstone blocks arranged as we see them today. Some of these blocks weighed 49 tons (50 t). They were brought from 25 miles (40 km) away.

The mystery remains

The real purpose of Stonehenge remains a mystery. The most popular theory is that it was used as an astronomical observatory to record the position of the sun. Stonehenge has suffered major damage from **erosion**. In the last 200 years it has also been damaged by humans. This world-famous structure is strictly protected and visitors are allowed to view it only from a distance.

▲ The stones that lie across the top of the upright blocks are exactly level, despite the sloping ground.

ZOOM IN

At Stonehenge, the grave of a man who died around 2300 B.C. was found. The arrowheads still in his body showed that he had been killed deliberately.

15

Brandenburg Gate

The Brandenburg Gate is a built construction that is famous for its construction and cultural importance. It was the most elaborate of a number of gates in the wall that was built around the city of Berlin in the late 1700s. It became the symbol of Germany throughout the world.

ZOOM IN

When the Brandenburg Gate was first built, only the royal family could use the widest, central entrance.

▼ The Brandenburg Gate was built as a symbol of peace and unity in Germany.

◄ The sculpture on the top of the gate is of a winged woman in a chariot drawn by four horses. She is Eirene, the goddess of peace.

Gate design

The design of the Brandenburg Gate was modeled on the gateway to the Acropolis of Athens, the site of the Parthenon. The gate is made up of six pairs of Greek-style columns. Each pair of columns is joined by a decorated panel. This makes five passageways through which people and traffic pass. On the top of the gate is a statue of Eirene, the goddess of peace, driving her chariot.

Gate of peace

Although the Brandenburg Gate was built to represent peace, it was later used to help divide Germany. It became part of the Berlin Wall, which closed off East Berlin from West Berlin for almost 30 years. The Brandenburg Gate is the only remaining gate of the old city wall that once surrounded Berlin. It is now the symbol of the freedom and joining together of the German people.

▲ The panels in between the columns are decorated with the adventures of Hercules, who fought many wars to try to achieve peace.

Roman Baths

FACT FINDER

Location **Bath, England, United Kingdom**

Date built **65 A.D.**

WORLD HERITAGE SITE **since 1987**

The Roman Baths is a collection of built structures that are famous for their construction and cultural importance. These public baths were built in England by the Romans more than 2,000 years ago. The city where they were built has since been called Bath. The Roman Baths are the only ones in the United Kingdom.

Original construction

Originally the Roman Baths had a timber roof, but later, a tile and concrete roof was built. The **complex** consists of the Great Bath, the Sacred Spring, and the temple of Sulis Minerva, a goddess with the power to heal the sick. Most of the structure now around the Great Bath was added in the 1700s and 1800s.

ZOOM IN
Public baths were important in Roman society as a place to relax and meet socially. People not only bathed, but also chatted and ate snacks.

 Bathing in the waters of the Great Bath was thought to bring good health. It was also supposed to help conditions such as arthritis and skin problems.

The Sacred Spring

The Sacred Spring supplies the Great Bath with natural hot water from an underground spring. The water is fed into the bath by drains.

The Roman Baths were sacred to the Romans. They threw offerings for themselves and **curses** against their enemies into the Sacred Spring to ask for Minerva's help. The Roman Baths were part of everyday life for the Romans, who ruled England at the time. They are an important part of the cultural history of the United Kingdom.

▲ Hot spring water flows from this ancient Roman pipe. The minerals in the water stain the drain an orange color.

ZOOM IN
The curses written to Minerva were often written backwards to give the writing magical properties.

Danube River

FACT FINDER

Location **eastern Europe**

Length **1,770 miles (2,850 km)**

The Danube River is a natural feature that is famous for its size. It is the second longest river in Europe and it carries more water than any other river in Europe. The Danube passes through nine countries. It rises in south-western Germany and flows into the Black Sea in Romania.

ZOOM IN
Pollution threatens wildlife in the river regions and makes the water undrinkable, especially in the lower regions.

In three parts

The Danube River has three main sections. In the first section, from the Black Forest to Hungary, the river flows very quickly. It never completely freezes over. In the middle section, from Hungary to Romania, it flows more slowly. The surface can freeze completely in Winter. In the third section, from Romania through the **delta**, or wetland area, to the Black Sea, the river flows even more slowly. Only some parts of this section freeze in Winter.

◄ In Hungary, the largest amount of water flows in April because the snow has melted and the spring rains have started.

A long history

Humans have been living in the Danube River region for the last 7,000 years. Several countries have built **hydroelectric stations** along the river to generate electricity. Over the years, however, factories have **polluted** the river by dumping **toxic waste** into it. Steps are being taken by the governments to reverse the damage that has been done to this famous river, and to prevent it from happening again.

▲ The city of Regensburg, Germany, is the most northern point of the Danube. This is the earliest surviving bridge over the Danube River.

ZOOM IN
The Danube delta is an important breeding area for fish and birds. It is Europe's largest wetland.

Colosseum

FACT FINDER

Height 157 feet (48 m)

Length 640 feet (195 m)

Width 525 feet (160 m)

Date built 72–80 A.D.

The Colosseum is a built structure that is famous for its construction and its antiquity. This **amphitheater** was built using a new method of the time, where the strength of the building depended on its foundations and not on its walls. The Colosseum was used for celebrations and sporting spectacles. It is especially famous for holding fights to the death between special fighters who were called **gladiators**.

ZOOM IN
The corridors that led to the seats in the Colosseum and the many gates meant that the whole building could be emptied in three minutes.

▼ The Colosseum was used for entertainment. Special celebrations went all day for many days.

► The Colosseum could seat 50,000 people.

Huge structure

The Colosseum is four stories high. Each of the first three stories consists of 80 arches separated by piers. The top storey is solid stone with small windows. The Colosseum also had chambers under the ground where the gladiators and animals were caged before the games.

Built to last

The Colosseum was built by highly skilled craftsmen. They built drains as far as 26 feet (8 m) underground. The concrete foundations are 39 to 42 feet (12–13 m) deep in some places. The use of open arches instead of solid walls meant that the foundations had less weight to support. Over the years, the Colosseum has been damaged by earthquakes and fire. These days, air pollution eats into the stonework. The Italian Government is continually undertaking restoration work to preserve what is left of this famous structure.

ZOOM IN
A maze of chambers and cages under the stadium floor held prisoners and wild animals who were about to fight.

emperor and officials

women and poor people

wealthy citizens

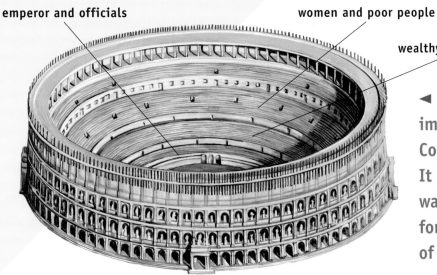

◄ This is an artist's impression of how the Colosseum used to look. It shows how the seating was divided into sections for the different levels of society.

City of Venice

FACT FINDER

Location Italy

Height 157 feet (48 m)

Size 1.7 square miles (4.5 sq km)

Date built 800–1700 A.D.

WORLD HERITAGE SITE since 1987

The historic city of Venice is a collection of built structures that are famous for their construction, antiquity and cultural importance. Most of the city of Venice is built on islands. Its age and its unique construction make it one of the most important **heritage cities** in Italy. Many of Venice's buildings are built on the top of wooden **piles** driven into the hard clay under the water. Venice has some streets, but the people mostly use the intricate system of **canals** to travel around the city.

ZOOM IN
Until 1854, there was only one bridge, the Rialto, across the Grand Canal.

Cultural centre

Over the years, Venice has become known as one of the cultural centres of the world. There are around 450 palaces and grand old houses, some of which still belong to the original families. The Doges' Palace, the palace from which the Doge, or Duke, of Venice ruled, was built in the 800s. It has been replaced and extended many times.

◄ Most of the city of Venice was built on islands. Canals in the heart of Venice separate the islands and take the place of streets.

◄ The Bridge of Sighs joins the Doges' Palace to the prison. This walkway was enclosed to prevent prisoners jumping from it on their way to prison.

► Part of a canal was filled in to build Saint Mark's Square. The square is the centre of public life in the city.

Threat to Venice

Today, the water that makes Venice unique has become a threat to its existence. Floods are becoming more serious and are causing the foundations to collapse. Many of the buildings are slowly sinking. Air pollution is also damaging the stone and marble. An international operation backed by the United Nations is now underway to rescue this world-famous city.

ZOOM IN
Originally, part of Saint Mark's Square was an orchard.

Parthenon

The Parthenon is a built structure that is famous for its construction and its antiquity. The building of the Parthenon was the work of the whole city. Citizens, slaves, and even foreigners living in the city worked on its construction. The ancient Greeks built this temple in thanks to the goddess, Athena. Athena was the guardian of the city of Athens, and the Greeks believed that she helped them in their battles to defend the city.

▼ The columns of the Parthenon lean inwards. This makes them look straight to the human eye.

► Sculptures are carved above the entrance columns of the temple. Many people believe that these represent the men who lost their lives in battle.

High city

The Parthenon stands on the rock of the Acropolis (which means "high city"). This was where only the most important temples stood. Most of the Parthenon was made of white marble. It is estimated that 21,648 tons (22,000 t) of marble were used in its construction. The Parthenon stands on a platform surrounded by 46 columns. Each column was made in 10 or 11 separate, drum-shaped pieces. These pieces were fitted together by metal or wooden pins that held them in place.

Art treasures

The Parthenon was once the home to some of the finest sculptures ever made. A 39-foot-(12-m) -high gold and ivory statue of Athena stood in the main part of the temple. This statue has since been destroyed. Carvings into the stone around the walls still remain. The Parthenon is the most important and most famous monument of ancient Greek civilization.

ZOOM IN
The Parthenon was thought to be Athena's home. Many religious celebrations were held outside so they would not trouble her.

INSIDE STORY

According to ancient Greeks, Athena was a goddess who had special powers to protect the city of Athens from harm. Athena was fully grown and armed with her shield when she was born. She was the goddess of wisdom, war, and crafts. Ancient Greeks believe it was Athena who invented the potter's wheel, showed Greeks how to grow the olive, and showed women how to weave.

Kremlin

FACT FINDER

Location Moscow, Russia

Size 28 hectares (69 ac)

Date built begun in 1147

WORLD HERITAGE SITE
  since 1990

The Kremlin is a collection of built structures that are famous for their construction, antiquity, and cultural importance. In 1147, part of the city of Moscow was surrounded by **fortifications**. It is this area that later became known as the Kremlin. Since 1992, the Kremlin has been the official residence of the president of Russia.

▼ The brick and stone walls were built to protect the people and buildings inside.

◄ The Assumption Cathedral is the oldest and largest temple in the Kremlin.

Walled city

The fortress-like walls and towers of the Kremlin that were built in the 1300s were white. In the late 1400s, the walls were completely rebuilt in red brick. These brick walls are more than 59 feet (18 m) high and are nearly 1.2 miles (2 km) long. Altogether, there are 20 towers built into the walls, mostly at the corners and various entrances.

▲ Ivan the Great's Bell Tower is the tallest structure in the Kremlin.

Important buildings

Inside the Kremlin are many important buildings that have been built over the last 600 years. These include churches, monasteries, palaces, military quarters, gardens, **tombs** of famous past leaders, and government administration buildings.

The Kremlin is one of the largest architectural complexes in the world. It is also the home of Russia's historical records and its greatest cultural treasures and art works.

ZOOM IN
The Kremlin gets its name from the Russian word *kreml,* which means "fortress."

Famous places of Europe

Our world has a rich collection of famous places. Some are spectacular natural wonders and some are engineering or architectural masterpieces. These famous places in Europe are outstanding in many different ways.

Wonders formed by nature

PLACE	FAMOUS FOR
Mont Blanc	The tallest mountain in western Europe
Danube River	The second longest river in Europe Carries more water than any other river in Europe Passes through nine countries

Masterpieces built by humans

PLACE	FAMOUS FOR
Eiffel Tower	The symbol of Paris, France, throughout the world One of the first steel and wrought-iron towers ever built
Little Mermaid	The symbol of Copenhagen, Denmark, throughout the world
Alhambra	One of the world's greatest examples of Islamic architecture
Stonehenge	One of the oldest monuments in Europe
Brandenburg Gate	The only remaining gate of the old city wall that once surrounded Berlin
Roman Baths	The only Roman Baths in England
Colosseum	The symbol of Rome, Italy, throughout the world
City of Venice	A city built on a number of islands Transport is mostly via a system of canals
Parthenon	The world's most important monument of ancient Greek civilization
Kremlin	One of the largest fortified group of buildings in the world The symbol of the Moscow, Russia, throughout the world

Glossary

amphitheater a round building with an open area in the middle and raised seats all around it

canals artificial waterways used by ships and to provide water to farms

centenary a 100-year anniversary

chambers compartments or enclosed spaces

complex a group of buildings

continent one of the main land masses of the world

curses wishes or prayers that something evil will happen to someone else

delta the flat, very fertile land near the mouth of a river

erosion the breaking down and wearing away by the elements of the weather, such as water, wind, and ice

fortifications walls or a fort built to protect from enemy attack

girders thick metal beams used as supports in building

glaciers large areas of snow that become hard like ice and move slowly down a mountain

gladiators specially trained fighters in ancient Rome who fought as entertainment

heritage cities cities that are kept in their original condition because they are important to that country's cultural history

hydroelectric stations factories set up to produce electricity using falling water as a source of power

piles long, heavy poles driven into the ground to help support a building

polluted spoiled or made dirty

pylons tall, tower-like structures

sultans the rulers of a Muslim country

summit the top or highest point

tombs graves, especially for important people

toxic waste leftover industrial products that are poisonous

vegetation the plant life of a particular area

wrought-iron a type of iron that is easy to bend and work with

Index